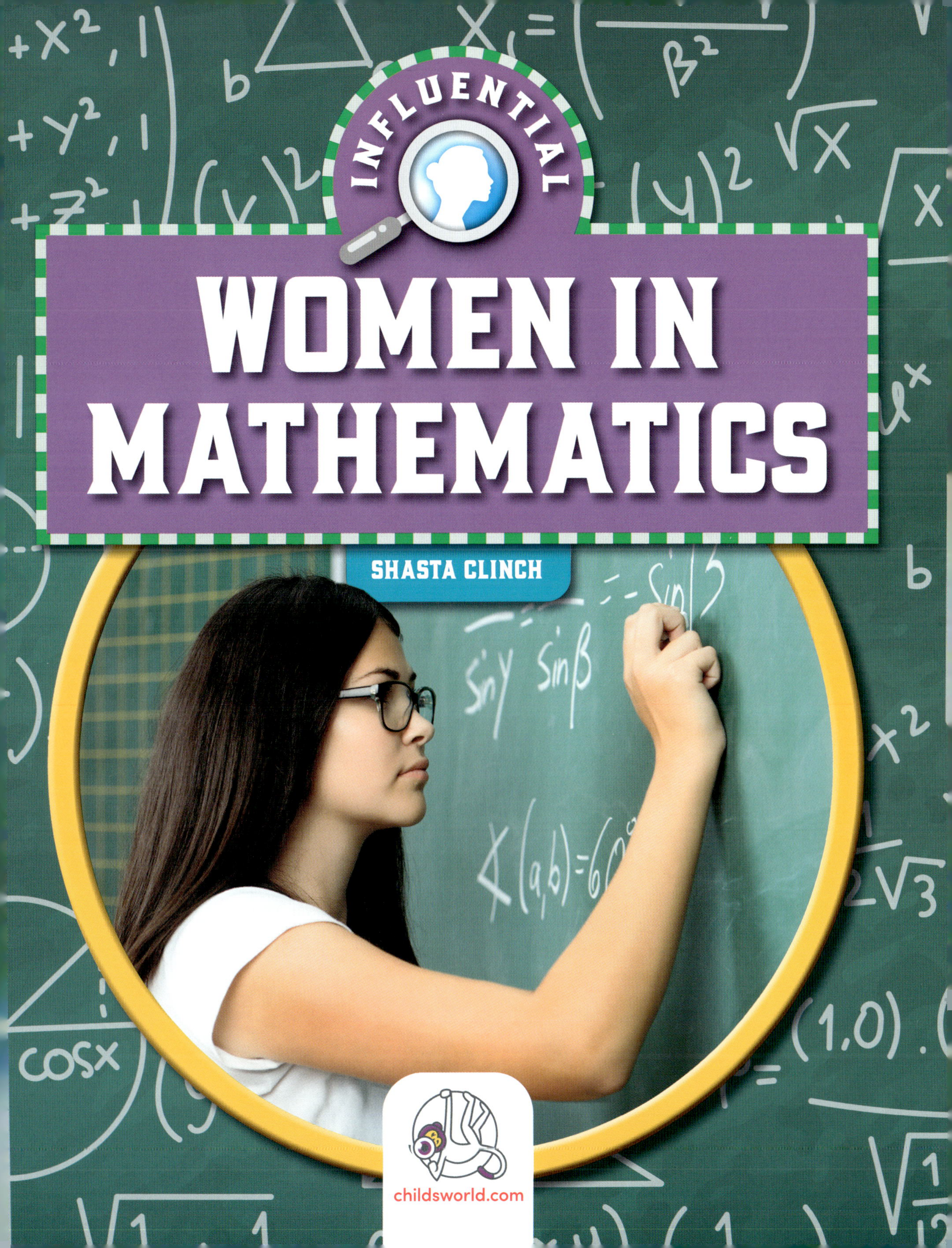
INFLUENTIAL
WOMEN IN
MATHEMATICS
SHASTA CLINCH
childsworld.com

Published by The Child's World®
800-599-READ • www.childsworld.com

Photography Credits
Photographs ©: Shutterstock Images, cover (foreground), cover (background), 1 (foreground), 1 (background), 3 (background), 7, 8–9, 15, 22; Alexander Skowalsky/Noun Project, cover (icon), 1 (icon), 3 (icon), back cover; Science History Images/Alamy, 5; Bill Ingalls/NASA, 11; Pictures From History/Newscom, 13; Leonardo Cendamo/Hulton Archive/Getty Images, 17; Vespasian/Alamy, 18; Red Line Editorial, 20

ISBN Information
9781503889606 (Reinforced Library Binding)
9781503890275 (Portable Document Format)
9781503891517 (Online Multi-user eBook)
9781503892750 (Electronic Publication)

LCCN 2023950192

Printed in the United States of America

Shasta Clinch is a freelance copy editor and proofreader. She lives with her husband and two lovely littles in New Jersey.

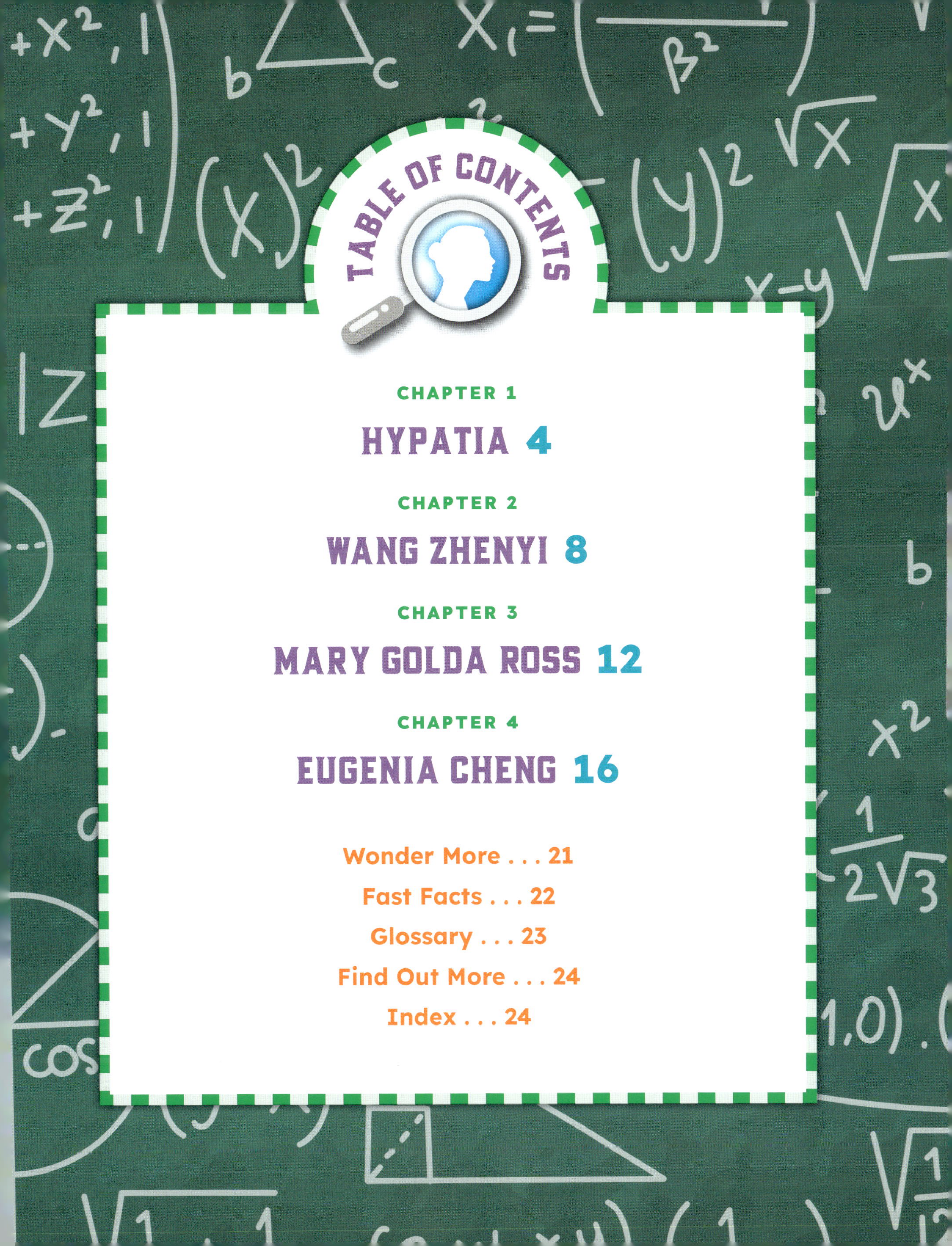

TABLE OF CONTENTS

CHAPTER 1

HYPATIA 4

CHAPTER 2

WANG ZHENYI 8

CHAPTER 3

MARY GOLDA ROSS 12

CHAPTER 4

EUGENIA CHENG 16

Wonder More . . . 21

Fast Facts . . . 22

Glossary . . . 23

Find Out More . . . 24

Index . . . 24

HYPATIA

Hypatia (hih-PAH-tyah) was born in Alexandria, Egypt, in the mid-300s AD. Back then, most women were taught how to care for their home and family. But Hypatia's father was a famous **mathematician** and librarian. He taught her the way he would have taught a son. He made sure she learned mathematics and **astronomy**. Hypatia helped her father with his work. Soon she became an expert at math. She was one of the first female mathematicians.

People are not sure exactly what year Hypatia was born.

Hypatia was also a famous teacher. She was very popular. People came from all over to learn from her. She was good at making math and astronomy easy to understand. This allowed her teachings to survive for a long time. She studied numbers and geometry, the field of math about shapes. Her work helped future mathematicians. They used her work to come up with new ideas. She also taught people how to use the astrolabe. People used this tool for hundreds of years. It helped them figure out where they were by measuring the positions of stars.

Hypatia's work proved that math was not just for men. Even though she lived around 1,700 years ago, some of her work survives to this day. Women today consider her an inspiration.

The word *astrolabe* means "star-taking" in Greek.

CHAPTER 2

WANG ZHENYI

Wang Zhenyi was born in 1768 in China. During this time, women could not go to school. But her family valued education. They worked together to teach her astronomy, poetry, medicine, geography, and mathematics. Wang was a quick learner. Soon she knew more than the rest of her family. Wang continued to teach herself. She even tried to read all the books in her grandfather's library.

Wang lived for part of her life in the city of Jiangning, now known as Nanjing.

Wang's best subjects were mathematics, astronomy, and poetry. She used her knowledge of math to figure out how objects moved in the night sky. Wang was one of the first Chinese **scholars** to correctly explain what caused **eclipses**. She was also an expert at trigonometry. This is the branch of mathematics about angles.

Wang understood how hard learning mathematics could be. She wrote a guide for beginners called *The Simple Principles of Calculation*. She explained important ideas about angles in her work, too. She wanted to make mathematics a subject that anyone could understand.

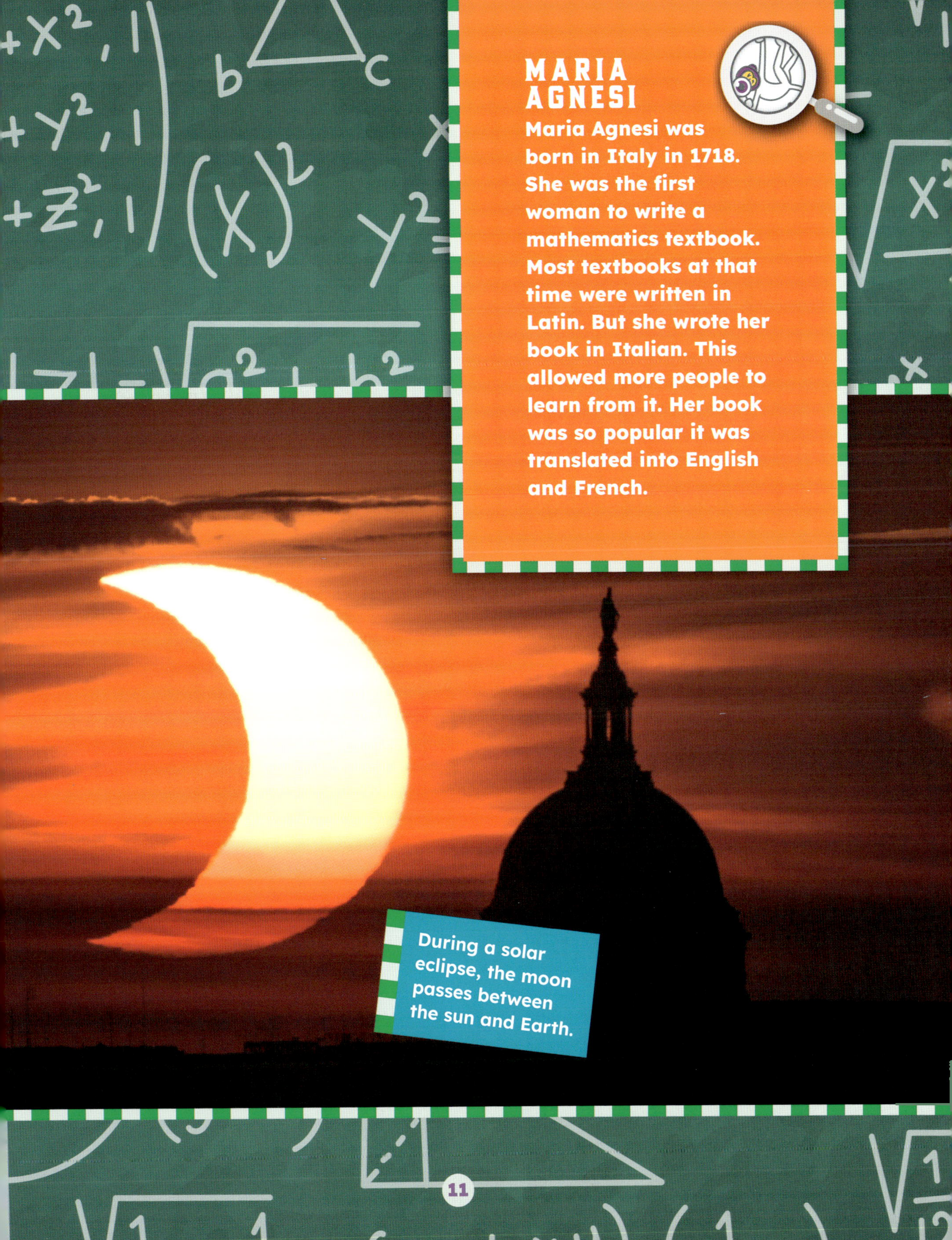

MARIA AGNESI

Maria Agnesi was born in Italy in 1718. She was the first woman to write a mathematics textbook. Most textbooks at that time were written in Latin. But she wrote her book in Italian. This allowed more people to learn from it. Her book was so popular it was translated into English and French.

During a solar eclipse, the moon passes between the sun and Earth.

MARY GOLDA ROSS

Mary Golda Ross was born in Park Hill, Oklahoma, in 1908. She was a member of the Cherokee Nation. At the time, girls were not expected to study math and science. But her parents wanted her to study those subjects anyway. They sent her to live with her grandparents in another town. There, she could go to school.

Ross taught math and science for almost 10 years.

Ross loved math. She felt that it was important to know math in the **modern** world. She became a math and science teacher. She also **mentored** Native American girls. She knew how important it was for them to have Native teachers.

World War II (1939–1945) started when Ross was 31. During the war, she got a job as a mathematician at Lockheed Aircraft Corporation. There, she designed fighter airplanes. She used **algebra**, geometry, and trigonometry. Her bosses noticed her skills. They gave her the chance to become an engineer. In 1949, Ross became the first Native American female **aerospace engineer**. She began working on spacecraft. Later, she joined a special group at Lockheed. She worked on secret military technology.

Ross knew that her Cherokee **heritage** was a big part of her success.

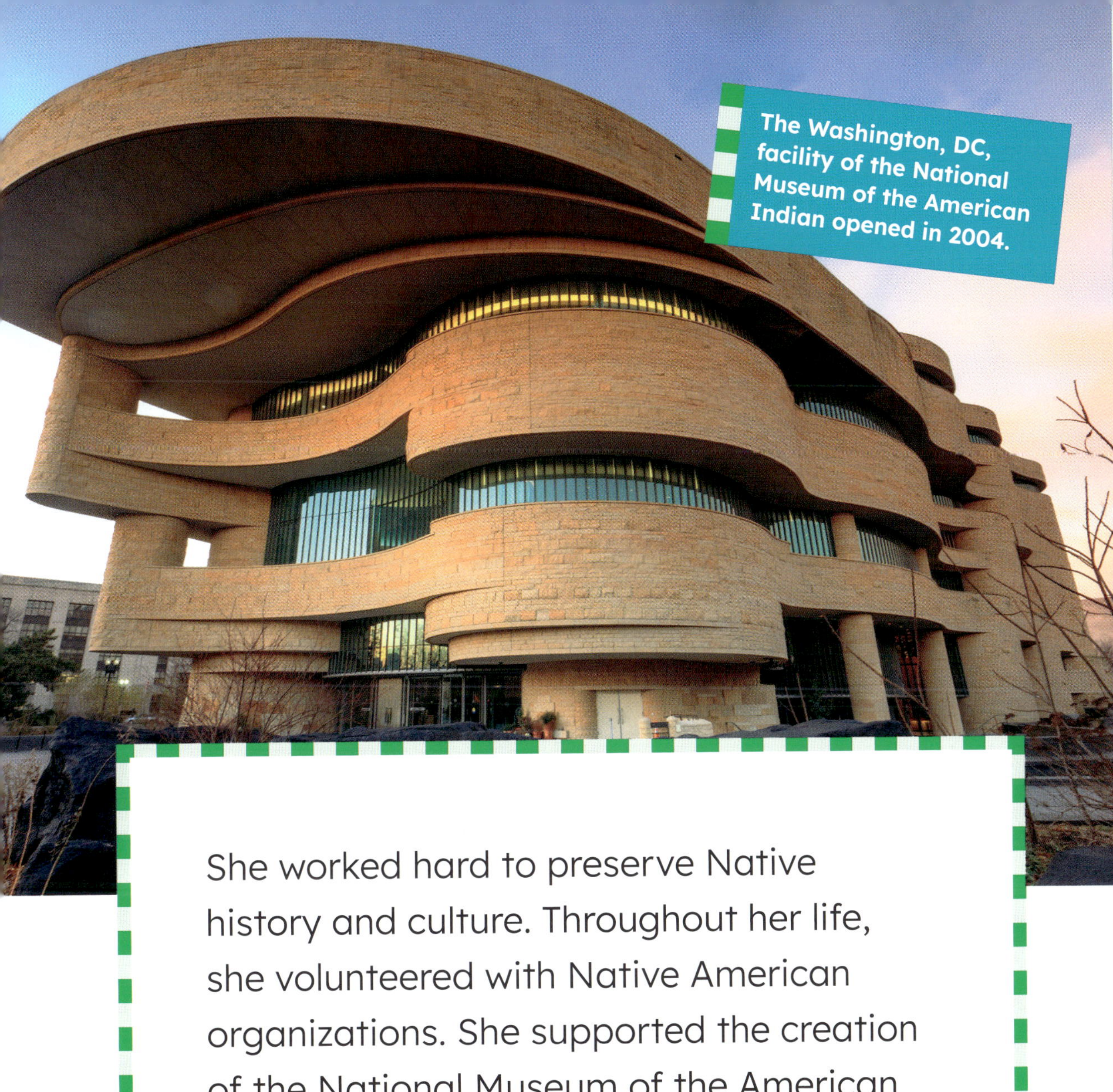

The Washington, DC, facility of the National Museum of the American Indian opened in 2004.

She worked hard to preserve Native history and culture. Throughout her life, she volunteered with Native American organizations. She supported the creation of the National Museum of the American Indian. After her death, Ross was honored with a special one-dollar coin. On the back of the coin was an illustration of her and a spaceship.

EUGENIA CHENG

Eugenia Cheng was born in England in the 1970s. Her parents were from Hong Kong. Sometimes she found it hard to fit in. She was often the only girl in her math classrooms. She learned to work hard. Cheng hoped that one day everyone would feel welcome in the field of mathematics.

Besides studying math, Cheng also plays the piano.

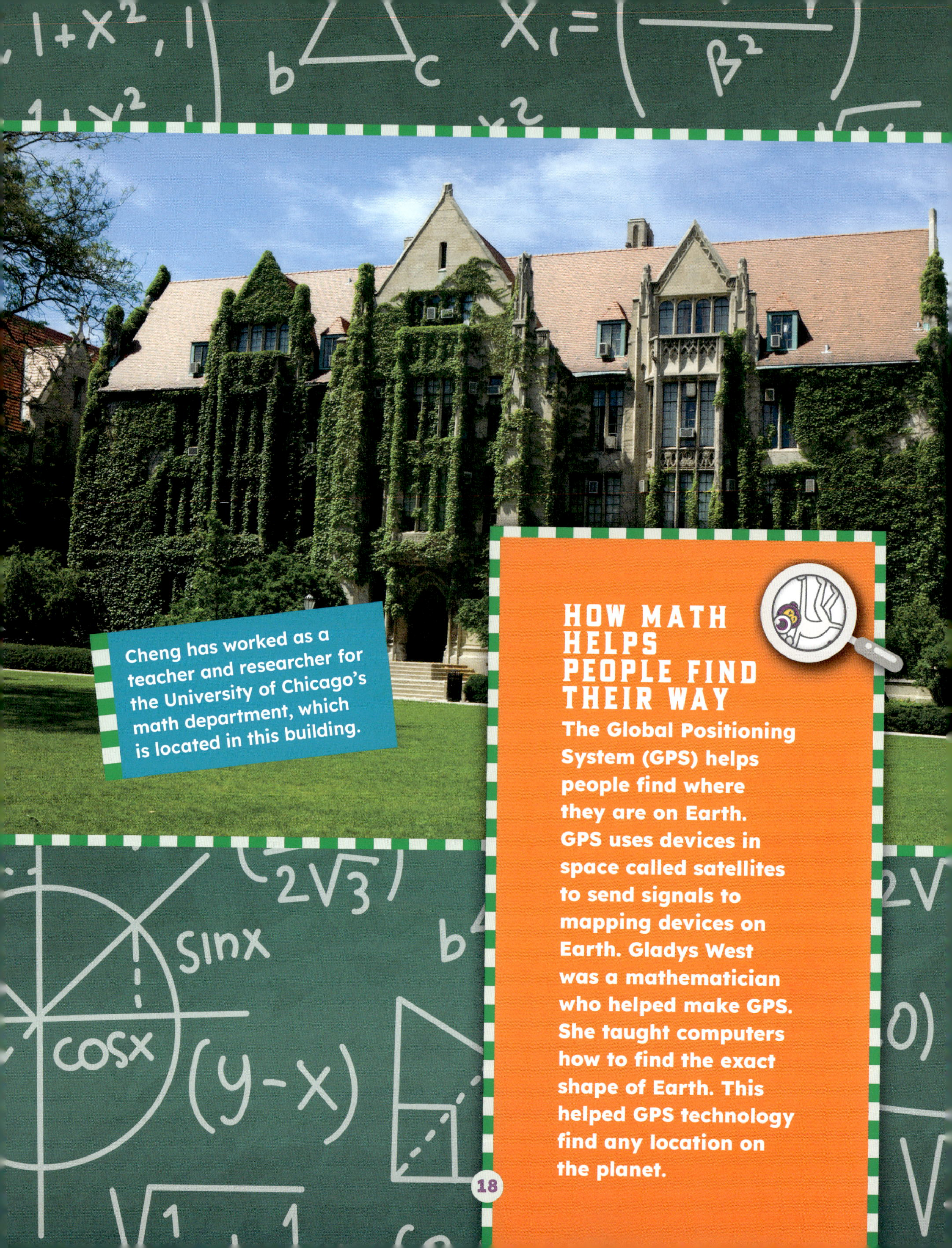

Cheng has worked as a teacher and researcher for the University of Chicago's math department, which is located in this building.

HOW MATH HELPS PEOPLE FIND THEIR WAY

The Global Positioning System (GPS) helps people find where they are on Earth. GPS uses devices in space called satellites to send signals to mapping devices on Earth. Gladys West was a mathematician who helped make GPS. She taught computers how to find the exact shape of Earth. This helped GPS technology find any location on the planet.

After studying math for several years, Cheng became a mathematician. Her research has focused on category theory. This is an advanced field of math that began in the mid-1940s. Cheng never forgot about wanting to make math more welcoming. She has worked to make difficult math concepts easier to understand. She has also used category theory to help explain social problems. For example, she has used math to make it easier to talk about gender.

Cheng has written several books. Her first was called *How to Bake Pi*. The title is a pun on the number pi, which is equal to about 3.14. The book explores how math is like baking. Both are about putting together ingredients to make new results.

HOW MANY MATH PROFESSORS ARE WOMEN?

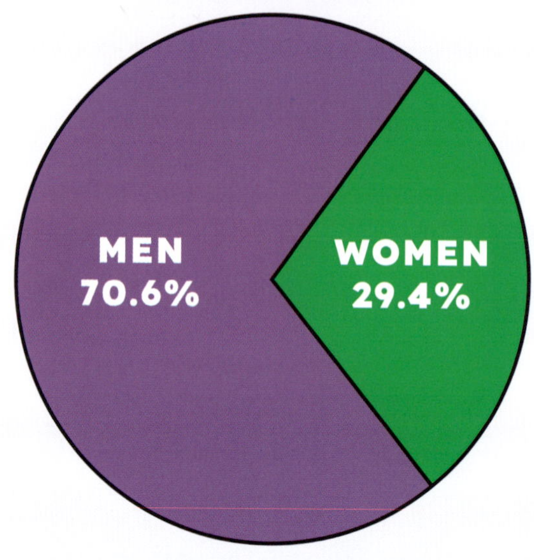

This pie chart shows what percentage of full-time, doctoral math professors in the United States were women in 2021.

Cheng has also worked as a mathematician at an art school. She taught math to artists. Many of those artists never cared about math. Cheng showed them that anybody can find something to like about mathematics.

WONDER MORE

Wondering about New Information

How much did you know about the history of women in mathematics before reading this book? What new information did you learn? Write down three new facts that this book taught you. Was the new information surprising? Why or why not?

Wondering How It Matters

What is one way mathematics relates to your life? If you cannot think of a personal connection, imagine a way math might affect other kids. What impact might it have on their lives?

Wondering Why

What is one way you use math daily? Can you think of a way you can use math to solve a problem you have?

Ways to Keep Wondering

There are many different kinds of mathematics. After reading this book, what questions do you have about math? Is there a field of mathematics that interests you?

FAST FACTS

- Mathematics can be used to solve problems. Many jobs require the use of math.
- Hypatia was the first well-known female mathematician.
- Hypatia studied numbers and geometry.
- Maria Agnesi was the first woman to write a math textbook.
- Mary Golda Ross was a member of the Cherokee Nation. She studied math from a young age.
- Ross used mathematics to work on spacecraft.
- Gladys West helped create the Global Positioning System (GPS).
- Eugenia Cheng works in a field of mathematics called category theory.
- Cheng wants to help non-mathematicians find something to love about math.

GLOSSARY

aerospace engineer (AYR-oh-spays en-juh-NEER) An aerospace engineer is someone who designs planes and spacecraft. Mary Golda Ross worked as an aerospace engineer.

algebra (AL-juh-bruh) Algebra is the field of mathematics about solving problems for unknown numbers. Mary Golda Ross used algebra in her work.

astronomy (uh-STRON-uh-mee) Astronomy is the study of outer space. Wang Zhenyi studied astronomy.

eclipses (ee-KLIPS-is) Eclipses happen when an object in space moves into the shadow of another object. Wang Zhenyi wrote about eclipses.

heritage (HAYR-uh-tij) A person's heritage is the culture passed down by the person's ancestors. Mary Golda Ross had Cherokee heritage.

mathematician (ma-thuh-muh-TI-shun) A mathematician is someone who studies mathematics. Eugenia Cheng is a mathematician.

mentored (MEN-tord) A person has mentored someone when she gives advice or guidance. Mary Golda Ross mentored Native American girls.

modern (MAH-durn) Modern means of the current time. Many modern jobs require knowledge of mathematics.

scholars (SKAH-lurz) Scholars are experts in a particular subject. Mathematicians are scholars.

FIND OUT MORE

In the Library

Dickmann, Nancy. *Exploring Space: Women Who Led the Way*. New York, NY: Children's Press, 2022.

Kaiser, Emma. *Influential Women in Engineering*. Parker, CO: The Child's World, 2025.

Sorell, Traci. *Classified: The Secret Career of Mary Golda Ross, Cherokee Aerospace Engineer*. Minneapolis, MN: Millbrook Press, 2021.

On the Web

Visit our website for links about women in mathematics:
childsworld.com/links

Note to Parents, Caregivers, Teachers, and Librarians: We routinely verify our web links to make sure they are safe and active sites. So encourage your readers to check them out!

INDEX

Agnesi, Maria, 11
algebra, 14
astrolabe, 6
astronomy, 4–6, 8–10

category theory, 19
Cheng, Eugenia, 16–20

eclipses, 10

geometry, 6, 14
GPS, 18

Hypatia, 4–7

National Museum of the American Indian, 15

pi, 19

Ross, Mary Golda, 12–15

trigonometry, 10, 14

Wang Zhenyi, 8–11